Mum's Tum

Written by
William Anthony

Illustrated by
Maia Batumashvili

Anna liked to think. She liked to think of this and that. She was thinking about Mum's tum.

Mum had a kid in her tum. The kid would be born soon.

Anna did not like the new kid. She did not want extra living with her.

Anna went to look for Mum. Mum was eating oats by the TV. Her tum was big.

"Mum," said Anna, "will the kid be a boy?"
"Do you think it will be a boy?" asked Mum.

"Ew! No boys!" said Anna. Anna had a think. "Do you need this new kid?"

"What are you asking that for?" said Mum.
"I want to send the kid back if it's rubbish," Anna moaned.

Anna was annoyed. The kid was going to be here soon. She went up to her room to think again.

Anna had a think about the kid. What if it was big? So big that it was bigger than her?

Anna did not like that. Anna was a big girl now, and she did not need the kid to be bigger than she was.

What if the kid had loads of arms and legs? What if the kid was an octopus?

Anna did not like that at all. An octopus has an awful lot of arms and legs.

Anna had a think. She went to ask Arjan. Arjan was good at helping.

"Arjan, do you think my Mum's new kid will be an octopus?" asked Anna.
"No," said Arjan.

Arjan was not much help at all. Arjan said that the kid might be a bot.

Anna did not like that. What if the kid said things like "beep zing borp thap"?

Anna asked Jack for help, too. He said the kid might be a bit of toast or a sandwich.

Anna liked toast. She might like the new kid after all. She had to think yet again.

Ella had a think for Anna. "What if the kid is an animal?" Ella asked.

Anna grinned a big grin. Anna liked them a lot. She had one last quick think.

Anna went back on the coach. She ran to tell Mum what she was thinking about the new kid.

Mum had left. Gran was sat on the chair.
"Mum has left for the kid," Gran said.

Gran took Anna to go and see the new kid.
"I think the kid will be an animal," said Anna.

"Do you?" asked Gran. "Shall we go and see?"
Gran and Anna went to look for Mum.

Mum was in bed with the new kid in her arms. It was not toast, an octopus or furry.

"This is Jenna," said Mum.
Anna looked at the kid and said, "Hello!"
The kid looked at Anna and said:

Mum's Tum

1. Why didn't Anna like the new kid in Mum's tum?

2. What was the first animal Anna worried the kid might be?

   (a) A lion

   (b) A bee

   (c) An octopus

3. What is the name of the new kid?

4. What words does the new kid say?

   Where in the story have you read those words before?

5. How do you think you would feel if you were Anna?

   Would you have done anything differently to Anna?

©This edition published 2023. First published in 2020.
BookLife Publishing Ltd.
King's Lynn, Norfolk, PE30 4LS, UK

ISBN 978-1-80155-994-2

A catalogue record for this book is
available from the British Library.

Mum's Tum
Written by William Anthony
Illustrated by Maia Batumashvili

An Introduction to BookLife Readers...

Our Readers have been specifically created in line with the London Institute of Education's approach to book banding and are phonetically decodable and ordered to support each phase of the Letters and Sounds document.

Each book has been created to provide the best possible reading and learning experience. Our aim is to share our love of books with children, providing both emerging readers and prolific page-turners with beautiful books that are guaranteed to provoke interest and learning, regardless of ability.

BOOK BAND GRADED using the Institute of Education's approach to levelling.

PHONETICALLY DECODABLE supporting each phase of Letters and Sounds.

EXERCISES AND QUESTIONS to offer reinforcement and to ascertain comprehension.

BEAUTIFULLY ILLUSTRATED to inspire and provoke engagement, providing a variety of styles for the reader to enjoy whilst reading through the series.

AUTHOR INSIGHT:
WILLIAM ANTHONY

Despite his young age, William Anthony's involvement with children's education is quite extensive. He has written over 60 titles with BookLife Publishing so far, across a wide range of subjects. William graduated from Cardiff University with a 1st Class BA (Hons) in Journalism, Media and Culture, creating an app and a TV series, among other things, during his time there.

William Anthony has also produced work for the Prince's Trust, a charity that helps young people with their professional future. He has created animated videos for a children's education company that works closely with the charity.

This book focuses on /oa/ and is a Green level 5 book band.